The Second Armada Book
of Jokes and Riddles

✝

PARISH OF DRUMRAGH
DIOCESE OF DERRY

This book was awarded to

ADELA ELLIS

in Class....*12*....for

ATTENDANCE
and
PROFICIENCY

in Sunday School for the year

ending June, 19..*85*.

Mr. W. J. E. Dukelow   D. C. Orr
Superintendent   Rector

Born in Cornwall, Jonathan Clements has in his lifetime been a gravedigger, Admiralty chart-compiler, dustman, artist, actor, roadsweeper, milk-man, poet, greengrocer, life-saver, photographer, advertising copywriter, footballer, singer – and, in all, had about two hundred jobs before he turned to writing. When he isn't writing children's books (and this is his sixth), he writes for magazines and throws Frisbees high in the air. His next project is to write a history of pickled onions, or a collection of mind-bending insults. Jonathan Clements lives on Salis-bury Plain in Wiltshire, and owns a rusty bicycle named Hortense.

Also by Jonathan Clements

The Armada Book of Jokes and Riddles
Crazy – But True!
More Crazy – But True!
Lucky For You!
The Great British Quiz Book

Other Armada Fun and Joke Books

The Awful Joke Book
The Even More Awful Joke Book
The Most Awful Joke Book Ever

The Funniest Funbook
The Batty Book Book
Edited by Mary Danby

The Trickster's Handbook
The Secret Agent's Handbook
The Whizzkid's Handbook
The Whizzkid's Handbook 2
The Whizzkid's Handbook 3
The Millionaire's Handbook
The Spookster's Handbook
by Peter Eldin

Jokes & Riddles from A–Z
by Bill Howard

The Second Armada Book of Jokes and Riddles

Compiled by Jonathan Clements
with drawings by Roger Smith

AN ARMADA ORIGINAL

The arrangement of this collection is
copyright © Jonathan Clements 1978

An Armada Original

First published in 1978
in Armada by Fontana Paperbacks,
8 Grafton Street, London W1X 3LA.

Armada is an imprint of Fontana Paperbacks,
a division of the Collins Publishing Group.

This impression 1985

Printed in Great Britain by
William Collins Sons & Co Ltd Glasgow

Conditions of Sale
This book is sold subject to the condition
that it shall not, by way of trade or otherwise,
be lent, re-sold, hired out or otherwise circulated
without the publisher's prior consent in any form of
binding or cover other than that in which it is
published and without a similar condition
including this condition being imposed on the
subsequent purchaser.

Contents

Jokes and Riddles to Start a Third World War

(*And Other Barmy Battles*)

One weapon that seems to have been overlooked by the masters of military madness is the awful joke, or its sister, the ridiculous riddle. Yet they can be more murderous than a missile, more lethal than a laser gun and more powerful than a pack of gelignite. So let's all campaign to scrap conventional weapons and use fatal doses of lunatic laughter. In this book you'll find an awesome armoury of jokes guaranteed to render the enemy helpless, and enough riddles to make whole armies run screaming off cliff-tops in their desire to escape. So memorise these jokes, then eat them. They're delicious on toast.

Two adventurers were sitting on a river bank in South America, dangling their feet in the stagnant water. Suddenly a vicious crocodile swam up and snapped a leg off one of them.

'I say,' drawled the unfortunate fellow to his companion. 'A crocodile just bit off my leg.'

'Really?' said his friend. 'Which one?'

The other intrepid adventurer yawned and replied: 'I don't know – you see one alligator and you've seen them all.'

At the inquest, the coroner gently asked the widow:

'Could you tell us what your late husband's last words were?'

'Yes,' she replied. 'He said: "I really don't see how they can make a profit out of selling this corned beef at ten pence a tin . . ."'

Unfamiliar with London traffic, a country rustic hopped on a bus at Waterloo and asked the conductor if the bus would take him to Oxford Street.

'Which part?' said the conductor.

'Why – all of me, of course!' cried the rustic.

Horace Hoop was having difficulty seeing things, so he went to an optician. After examining his eyes, the optician said:

'Hmmmmm, this looks bad. Have your eyes ever been checked before?'

'No,' said Horace. 'As far as I can remember, they've always been dark blue.'

Who was one of the strongest dictators?
Muscleny.

What did the health attendant say to his girl assistant?
'Hi, Jean.'

A pair of somewhat scatty teenage girls were crossing the Atlantic by boat for the very first time. As they leant on the rail, looking out at the ocean, one of them said:

'Gosh – look at all that water out there!'

'Yes, Mirabelle,' said her chum. 'And just think – that's only the *top* of it!'

A man walking along a country lane encou... lady who was holding two kettles up to her couldn't help asking her what she was doing.

'Well, if you hold two kettles to your ears,' the woman said, 'you can hear a noise like a football match.'

The man took the two kettles, held them up to his ears for a while, then said. '*I* can't hear anything.'

'Ha-ha!' cackled the old lady. 'It must be half-time . . .'

A rather dim lad called Harry Pole was idly leaning over the rail of Brighton pier when a woman fell over the rails in an effort to stop her hat blowing away. She landed *splash*! in the deep sea, and shouted to Harry above: 'For goodness sake, drop me a line!'

'OK,' said Harry. 'What's your address?'

DRINKER: Excuse me, do you know how to make a fresh peach punch?
BARMAN: Sure – give her boxing lessons.

In what ball can you carry your shopping?
A basketball.

s an eight-stone weakling,' the man said to his friend. 'Whenever I went to the beach with my girl friend, this fourteen-stone bully came over and kicked sand in my face. So I took the famous Charlie Universe body-building course. In just a short while I weighed fourteen stone and bulged with muscles.'

'And what happened?' his friend asked him.

'Well, I went to the beach with my girl friend and a twenty-one-stone bully kicked sand in my face.'

The Latin-American diplomat was describing his country to members of a women's knitting circle in Dorset.

'Our most popular sport is bull-fighting,' he declared.

One sweet old lady, obviously upset at the thought of so bloodthirsty a spectacle, said: 'But isn't that *revolting*?'

'No, madame,' said the Latin, with a wide smile, 'that is our *second* most popular sport.'

Why were seven wooden planks standing in a circle?
They were having a board meeting.

What did the Russian Tarzan say when he met a crane?
'*Me Tarzan. Ukraine.*'

What did the detective say when he'd finally tracked down the criminal?
'*I'm policed to meet you.*'

If a dog loses his tail, where does he get another?
At a re-tail shop.

Edwin Bootlegger was wakened from a deep sleep by a loud knocking at the door. He staggered out of bed, made his way to the front door and opened it. There he peered blearily at a woman collecting for charity.

'I say, I'm awfully sorry if I woke you up,' said the woman.

'Oh, that's all right,' yawned Edwin. 'I had to get up to answer the door, anyway.'

'May I be of help, sir?' asked the impeccably-attired, haughty salesman in the Rolls-Royce showroom.

'Yes, I think so,' said the rich customer. 'My girl friend isn't feeling very well. What have you got in the way of a get-well-soon car?'

A labourer on a building site had just started work. When the middle of the week came he found he was broke. So he went up to the manager of the site.

'Can I have my week's wages now?' he asked.

'But you've only been here three days!'

'I know,' the labourer agreed. 'But if I can trust you for the first half of the week, surely you can trust me for the second half!'

'Psychiatry is a lot of junk,' said one man to another.

'Oh?' said his companion. 'Why do you say that?'

'Well, today my psychiatrist told me that I'm in love with my umbrella. Have you ever heard of anything so silly?'

'It does sound rather daft.'

'I mean, me and my umbrella certainly have a sincere affection for each other. But *love*? That's just ridiculous!'

What kind of a motorbike can cook eggs?
A scrambler.

Why didn't the piglets listen to their father?
Because he was such a boar.

Why were the Colosseum managers in ancient Rome angry at their lions?
Because they were eating up all their prophets (profits).

On holiday in London, a married couple, both Indian fakirs, booked into a hotel. On their first night, the man was very tired and he gave a wide yawn.

   'Have you made the bed yet?' he asked his wife.

   'I can't,' she said. 'I forgot the nails.'

ARNOLD: What makes you think I'm so stupid?
AMANDA: Well, when you went to that mind-reader just now, she only charged you half-price!

HOTEL MANAGER: Well, Mr Sloop, did you enjoy your stay here with us?
GUEST: Yes, but I'm a bit upset about leaving the place so soon after I've practically bought it.

Where had the runner bean?
To see the celery stalk.

What did the cobbler say when a flock of chickens came into his workshop?
Shoo!

POLITICIAN: Tell me, how do you know when a person is insane?

PSYCHIATRIST: Well, firstly I ask them questions that an average person can answer easily. For example: If Captain Cook made five trips around the world and was killed on one of them – which one was it?

POLITICIAN: Er . . . Well . . . Couldn't you ask me a question on another subject? I'm not very good at history.

The theatrical impresario Maxie Doldum was once approached by a man in his theatre.

'I've got an act to offer you that is really unique,' said the man. 'It will take London by storm. All you have to do is put £10,000 in the bank for my wife . . . and I'll commit suicide on the stage of your theatre.'

Somewhat astounded, Maxie pondered the offer. 'Hmmmmm,' he finally said. 'But what will you do for an encore?'

From which seafaring book can you get splinters?
A log-book.

An undertaker's assistant named Jerkins went to see his boss to ask for a rise. Jerkins mentioned that several big companies were after him.

'Oh – what companies?' his boss asked.

Jerkins replied: 'Well, there's the electricity company, the gas company, the hire-purchase company . . .'

Despite her husband's protests, Eliza Skippington insisted on taking a dozen large suitcases of clothes with them on holiday. When they arrived at the station to leave, loaded with luggage, Walter Skippington groaned, 'You know, we might have brought the piano with us as well.'

'There's no need to be sarcastic,' snapped Eliza.

'I'm not being sarcastic,' said Walter. 'I left the tickets on top of it.'

A nuclear physicist went into a chemist's shop and asked the assistant: 'Could I have some prepared acetyl-salicylic acid, please?'

'Do you mean aspirin?' said the assistant.

'Yes, that's the stuff,' said the physicist. 'I can never remember its name.'

Where do geologists put their samples?
In their rock-sacks.

A dollar and a cent fell out of a pocket. The cent rolled along the gutter and fell down a drain. Why didn't the dollar follow?
It had more cents (sense).

SPOT THE DIFFERENCE

NOAH'S ARK
(made of wood)

JOAN OF ARC
(maid of Orleans)

What's the difference between Noah's Ark and Joan of Arc?
One was made of wood, and the other was Maid of Orleans.

101 Things to Make out of Truly Terrible Jokes and Riddles

(*How to Create Confusion and Be Considered Creative*)

Just what can you make? Well, for a start you can make a thorough nuisance of yourself, simply by telling the jokes and asking the riddles. Using the same technique, you can make strong men weep, fearless females flee in fright, and even cats hide in dustbins. You can also make yourself a fortune (well, a few miserable pennies at least) by memorising all the jokes, standing on an orange box and calling yourself Claude the Champion Comedian. Last of all, and by all means least, you can make a rather snazzy hat out of the book, sticking the pages together with prune-juice, and wearing it to public executions and garden fêtes. See how useful this book is turning out to be?

JUDGE: You are accused of driving at fifty miles an hour in a built-up area. How do you plead?

MOTORIST: Innocent. Look, your honour, I wasn't doing fifty, I wasn't doing forty, I wasn't doing thirty, I –

JUDGE: Careful, man, careful. You'll be backing into something in a minute.

The wife of a London bank hold-up man visited her husband in Wandsworth Prison, where he was serving his sentence. Through the wire grille he glared at her and whispered:

'The money, Flora – is it still *safe?*'

'Of course it is, Muggy,' she said. 'Now don't you worry about it any more. It couldn't be safer than the place where you buried it. They've gone and built a 25-storey block of flats on top of it!'

1ST COWBOY: Did you know they call you 'Paleface' on the reservation?
2ND COWBOY: No – why's that?
1ST COWBOY: Because you have a face like a bucket.

Two partners of a big American business were on a fishing trip when a sudden storm capsized their boat. One could swim, but the other floundered hopelessly.

'Nathaniel!' cried the swimmer. 'Can you float alone?'

'Look, Clancy,' gasped the non-swimmer, fighting for breath, 'this is no time to start talking business!'

What's the difference between an auction sale and being seasick?
One is the sale of effects and the other is the effects of a sail.

Why are some plants like very naughty boys?
Because they need a stick to grow up straight.

Why do elephants chew camphor balls?
To keep moths away from their trunks.

Why did the hatstand in the hall?
Because it had nowhere to sit.

One day long ago a famous artist was walking down the street when he saw a very beautiful woman. He decided that he must paint a picture of her. The woman's name was Lisa, and after a lot of persuasion she agreed to have her portrait painted.

When she went to his studio, she complained about the heating, the discomfort of the chairs, the lighting, the way the pose she had to hold made her ache, the weakness of the wine . . . in fact she complained of everything.

So when the famous artist finished his painting he called it 'The Moaner Lisa'.

PSYCHIATRIST: You'll be glad to know that you haven't got an inferiority complex after all.
PATIENT: Really?
PSYCHIATRIST: Yes. The thing is, you *are* inferior!

Knock-knock.
Who's there?
Romeo.
Romeo who?
Romeo ver the river.

Two men met in the Labour Exchange. One said to the other: 'Did you get that job they sent you after?'

'No,' said the other. 'It turned out to be the post of a mortuary attendant.'

'What was wrong with that?'

'Well, I thought it was rather a dead-end job.'

MRS P.: Are you married?

MRS D.: Well, I *was*. I was married to the man who won the 5000-metres final at the last Olympics.

MRS P.: Oh, I am sorry. What happened – did you divorce him?

MRS D.: No. He ran out on me.

A somewhat mean man named Gulliver Blanche took his whole family to dinner at a large restaurant. It was a very large meal, and they were unable to eat it all. So Gulliver beckoned the waiter over and asked him: 'I say, do you think I could have a plastic bag for the leftovers? I'd like to take them home for the dog.'

'Gosh, Dad,' said his little son Horace. 'Are we going to get a *dog*?'

HOLIDAYMAKER: I say, have you saved many people this season?
LIFEGUARD: Oh, dozens.
HOLIDAYMAKER: And have you saved any girls?
LIFEGUARD: Yes – about twenty.
HOLIDAYMAKER: Really? Can I have one?

'My husband makes all my dresses,' said the enormously fat lady to a friend. 'Since he retired, I've saved an absolute fortune!'

'Really? I suppose he was a tailor or cutter before he retired?'

'Oh no,' said the fat lady. 'He was a meat-packer.'

Why did the pig swill?
Because it saw the barn dance.

FRED: Had a good holiday?
DAVE: No, it was rotten. Rained every single day.
FRED: Well, you managed to get a good sun-tan.
DAVE: That's not a sun-tan . . . It's *rust*!

A sheep farmer went to the vet and said he was having trouble with a ram who kept banging his head against a barn. The vet said that the ram probably had bad nerves, and that playing some music might help to soothe him.

Several weeks later the vet visited the farmer and found that the ram had died. 'Did you play some music for him?' said the vet.

'Certainly,' said the farmer.

'What did you play?'

'I played a record of Ella Fitzgerald singing "There Will Never Be Another You".'

Who is the dampest monarch on earth?
The Shower of Persia.

What dance do tin-openers do?
The Can-Can.

28

At a political rally, the candidate was trying to make a stirring speech, but was constantly being interrupted by a noisy heckler in the audience.

'Tell them all you know!' cried the heckler. 'It won't take very long.'

The politician glared back and proclaimed: 'I'll tell them all we *both* know – it won't take any longer.'

A man was roaming around the jungle with a notebook in his hand. After a while he was spotted by a tribe of cannibals, who took him back to their camp for the Chief's dinner.

After being placed in the cauldron, the Chief came to him and said: 'What was your occupation?'

'I was an assistant editor on a newspaper,' the man said.

The Chief replied: 'Oh well, cheer up – soon you'll be an Editor-in-Chief.'

A famous comedian was once sent to entertain the Prime Minister at a dinner party at No. 10 Downing Street. After he had been introduced to the politicians, the comedian said to the Prime Minister:

'I would like to tell you all the latest jokes, sir.'

'No need, no need,' sighed the Prime Minister. 'I have already appointed them in my Cabinet.'

What did the oil painting say to the wall?
First they framed me, then they hung me.

What bird will never have a vote in an election?
A mynah bird, because he's too young.

During an operatic concert at the Festival Hall, while the nervous soprano was fumbling her way noisily through her role in *Don Giovanni*, one man in the audience turned to his friend and whispered: 'What do you think of this singer's execution?'

'Oh, I'm all for it,' was the reply.

Showing some important tourists from England around his vast ranch, a wealthy Texan casually remarked that he had 4,000 head of cattle.

'Oh gosh,' said Lord Trout, 'I think I can go one better than you there, old chap. I have a herd of 5,000 cattle in my meadows back in Hertfordshire –'

The Texan drawled in reply: 'What I meant, your Lordship, was that I have 4,000 head of cattle in the freezer.'

Two rather dense fellows entered a pub in London and finding a table empty, started to play a game of snooker. After half an hour, neither of them had scored a point. One of them whispered to his companion:

'I know – let's cheat.'

'Cheat? How do you mean?'

'Well, let's take away the wooden triangle.'

Which town in Britain sells **bad meat**?
Oldham.

What illness do retired pilots get?
'Flu.

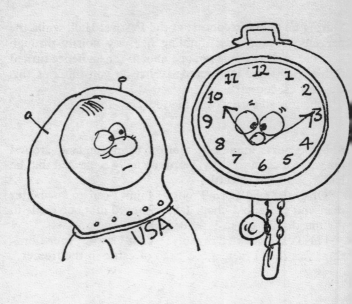

What will the first clock on the moon be called?
A luna-tick.

Which members of an orchestra can't you trust?
The fiddlers.

Two monsters met on a dark, evil night in the wilds of Transylvania. Having nothing in particular to do, one of them suggested to the other:

   'Like a game of "Vampires"?'

   'How do you play that?' said the other.

   'Oh, for very high stakes.'

What do cats strive for?
Purrfection.

Which two letters of the alphabet are corroded?
D. K. (*decay*)

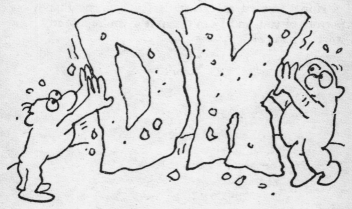

B

An obscure modern artist once showed his latest painting –
a big splosh of orange on the canvas with little black
blobs – to a prominent lady art critic.

'Well,' said the artist. 'What do you think of it?'

After staring in puzzlement and disgust at the picture
for a long time, the lady said: 'I'm afraid I must confess
that I think it's a pretty poor work of art.'

'Huh!' snorted the artist. 'It so happens that it's a
portrait of you, and I can't help it if you're a pretty poor
work of nature!'

Pete's Pet Shop

Do Armchairs Make Good Pets?

(No, and Neither Do Empty Pickled-Onion Jars)

Have you given serious thought lately to the notion of swapping your pet rat Rudyard for a pet riddle or a tame joke? No? Well, that's not surprising, presuming you're reasonably sane. But just consider the enormous advantages of having a pet riddle or joke as a pet – they're very clean in the house, eat only a few scraps, never bite your leg off (as do pet sharks), and don't demand to be taken for long walks along the railway track or play with pieces of electric wire. Next time you're in your local pet shop, ask the owner if he has any good pet riddles or jokes in stock. The chances are he won't, while you can fire hundreds at him . . .

In the bar of a swank hotel, the two richest men in the world met. The first bit into his caviare and sipped his gin, then drawled:

'You know, I've just decided to buy all the diamond and emerald mines in the world.'

The second man considered this for a moment, then quietly murmered: 'I'm not sure that I care to sell them.'

The Reverend Optimus Poke was an awful golfer. One day he shot a powerful drive from the green which disappeared into a large tree. The ball dropped down, then bounced and rolled towards the green; as if drawn by a magnet it continued rolling 200 yards towards the flag, and finally dropped right into the hole.

'Hole-in-one!' cried all the other golfers.

The Rev. Poke lifted his eyes towards heaven: 'Please Father,' he whispered, 'I'd rather do it myself.'

Why is an empty room like a room full of married people?
Because there isn't a single person in it.

What starts with T, ends with T, and is full of T?
A teapot.

What squeals more loudly than a pig caught under a fence?
Two pigs caught under a fence.

...ed quicker and shorter by
...em?

... in the Parachute Corps was showing a
g... ...its how to use their parachutes.

On... ...dier asked: 'But sir – what if the parachute
doesn't o...

The instructor smiled: 'That, my boy, is what is known
as jumping to a conclusion.'

JUDGE: You are charged with murder, burglary, loitering,
and knocking down a clump of trees.

PRISONER: Huh!

JUDGE: Well – how do you plead? Guilty or not
guilty?

PRISONER: Figure it out for yourself, mate – that's your
job, ennit?

Two small fish were swallowed by a whale. They bumped into each other while wandering about in the whale's dark innards.

The first small fish said: 'What's a nice sole like you doing in a plaice like this?'

The second fish said: 'Eel by gum, I don't know.'

Which particular dance do cleaners do?
The Char-Char.

POLICEMAN: I'm afraid that I'm going to have to lock you up for the night.

MAN: What's the charge?

POLICEMAN: Oh, there's no charge. It's all part of the service.

What do you get when you cross a donkey with a mother?
Ass-ma.

Which two types of fish do you need to make a shoe?
Sole and 'eel.

Three men stood before a judge on a charge of drunk and disorderly conduct in a public park.

JUDGE: What were you doing?

1ST MAN: Oh, just throwing peanuts in the pond.

JUDGE: And what were you doing?

2ND MAN: I was throwing peanuts in the pond, too.

JUDGE: Sounds harmless. And you, were you throwing peanuts in the pond as well?

3RD MAN: No, sir. I *am* Peanuts!

A woman walked into a smart dress shop and said to an assistant: 'Would you mind taking that pink dress with the orange ribbons out of the window for me?'

'Certainly, madam,' said the assistant. 'I'll fetch it.'

'Thank you,' said the woman. 'The wretched thing annoys me every time I pass!'

41

A tourist in London saw an advertisement for a restaurant which claimed that any dish requested could be served, no matter how strange or exotic.

The man decided to visit the restaurant in order to see how true the claim was. When he was seated at a table he asked for gorilla and chips. The waiter took this order calmly, and went away into the kitchen.

A short while later the waiter returned and said: 'I'm awfully sorry, sir, but we seem to have run out of potatoes.'

The eminent surgeon, Sir Lauderdale Flitch, was strolling through his local churchyard one day when he saw Tom Lurk, the gravedigger, having a rest and swigging from a bottle of beer.

'Hey, you!' called Sir Lauderdale. 'How dare you laze about and drink alcohol in the churchyard. Get on with your job or I shall tell the vicar.'

'I should have thought you'd be the last person to complain,' said Tom, 'bearing in mind all your blunders I've had to cover up.'

Why has a horse got six legs?
Because he has forelegs in front and two legs behind.

Take away my first letter, then my second, then my third, fourth and fifth letters, and I remain the same. What am I?
A postman.

Why did all the opticians go to the World Fair?
Because it was a spectacle.

Why is a fish shop always crowded?
Because the fish fillet.

What dance do vampires do?
The Fangdango.

'My biggest problem is that I always dream about cricket,'
said the man to his psychiatrist. 'Always about cricket.'
   'Don't you ever dream about girls?' said the doctor.
   'What – and miss my turn to bat!'

MAN: What do you do for a living?
GIRL: I'm a pin-up girl.
MAN: You mean you pose for photographs?
GIRL: Oh, no. It's just that I'm allergic to elastic.

One bright sunny morning, Mrs Malone turned to her husband and said: 'You know, Sidney, I think I'll take little Bertram to the zoo today.'

Mr Malone shrugged: 'I wouldn't bother if I was you. If they want the little devil, let them come and collect him.'

CUSTOMER: I'm looking for something cheap and nasty to give my mother-in-law as a present.
SHOPKEEPER: I've got just the thing, sir. You can have my father-in-law!

'Name the elements, Richard,' instructed the teacher.

'There's earth and there's air,' began the boy. 'And there's fire and er – oh yes, golf.'

The teacher stared in puzzlement: 'What on earth made you include that fourth item?'

'Well, miss,' said Richard, 'I overheard my mother telling one of her friends that when my father plays golf, he's in his element.'

The millionaire Texas oil-man went to see his dentist.

'And which tooth seems to be bothering you, Mr Crabmuncher?' the dentist asked him.

'Oh, just drill anywhere,' drawled the oil-man, 'I feel lucky today!'

BRENDA: Guess what happened when I washed my budgie in Omo.
BERNARD: What?
BRENDA: It died.
BERNARD: Well, I did tell you that Omo wasn't good for budgies.
BRENDA: Oh, it wasn't the Omo that killed it – it was the spin-dryer.

'Something the matter?' asked the café owner of the young well-dressed customer who sat staring glumly at his coffee.

'Well,' said the man, 'two months ago my grandfather died and left me £40,000.'

'That doesn't sound like anything to get upset about,' said the café owner.

'And last month an uncle I'd never even met passed away and left me £100,000.'

'So why are you looking so unhappy?'

'Well,' said the man, 'this month – so far – *nothing*!'

Why do many people go in for carpentry?
Because they think it's all plain (plane) sailing.

1ST MAN: Every day my dog Towser and I go for a tramp in the woods.
2ND MAN: Really? And does your dog enjoy it?
1ST MAN: Yes – but the tramp's getting a bit fed up with it.

The somewhat dumb but pretty girl in the bank stood at the window of the cashier's desk and smiled.

'I'd like to cash this cheque, please,' she said, handing it over.

The clerk examined the cheque, then said: 'Could you identify yourself, Miss?'

For a moment the lovely girl's brow creased over, then with a bright look she fumbled in her handbag and producing a mirror, glanced in it and with relief said, 'Yes – it's me, all right!'

PERCY: I have no trouble at all leaping out of bed as soon as the first ray of sunshine peeps through my bedroom window.
CECIL: Really? How energetic.
PERCY: I wouldn't say that. My bedroom faces west.

PATIENT: My hair keeps falling out. Can you suggest anything to keep it in?
DOCTOR: How about a carrier bag?

The door of the doctor's surgery burst open and a man rushed in. He was in a great state of agitation.

'Doctor,' he cried, 'you've got to help me. I think I'm losing my mind – I can't remember anything . . . not what happened a year ago, or even a day ago. I must be going crazy!'

'Hmmm,' said the doctor. 'Just when did you first become aware of this problem?'

The man looked puzzled. 'What problem, doctor?'

Jokes and Riddles
as Great Literature

(Or, *Art Ain't All Paint*)

What have the following famous writers in common: Byron, Shelley, Keats, Shakespeare, Conan Doyle, Maud Spangleknees, Tennyson, Salvation Quirk, Wordsworth, Charles Dickens? Correct – they all had feet. Another thing which united them was their fondness for the daft jest. Recently this scrap of conversation was discovered in the Goat Room of the British Museum:

Byron: I say, I say – what do owls sing when it's raining hard?

Shelley: She walks in beauty like the night –

Byron: No, Percy, you great fool. The owl sings: 'To-wet-to-woo.'

Shelley: What?

Byron: Blimey, I despair of making a great poet out of you, Perce.

So you see what illustrious company you keep, in sobbing hysterically over the jokes and riddles that are to come.

MAN: I'd like you to see my wife – I think she's insane.
PSYCHIATRIST: Oh, what makes you think that?
MAN: Well, she's just bought a hundredweight of steel wool.
PSYCHIATRIST: That's not evidence of insanity.
MAN: I know – but she's started knitting an electric cooker with it!

Young Sidney Spleen was surprised when his fiancée wrote to him calling their engagement off, and asking for her photo back. But not so surprised as she was when she received a large packet, containing about fifty photographs of girls, with the enclosed note:

'Dear Dolly – Can't remember which photo is yours – will you please sort it out and return the rest?'

Two rather stingy Scotsmen were comparing ways they had cut the cost of doing things.

'I run behind taxis to save more money,' boasted one.

'That's nothing,' said the other. 'I get all my grass cut for nothing and I don't have to lift a finger.'

'That's marvellous,' said the first. 'Tell me, how do you manage to do that.'

'Well, I've got this beastie with two horns that gives milk. I call it my lawn-mooer.'

How do you spell contentment in four letters?
A.P.N.S. (Happiness)

What time of day was Adam created?
A little before Eve.

What do you get if you cross a zebra with an ape-man?
Tarzan stripes forever.

51

CUSTOMER: Waiter! This chop is very tough.
WAITER: Yes, sir, it's probably a karate chop.
CUSTOMER: Well, have you got pig's trotters?
WAITER: No, sir – flat feet.

BILL: The police are looking for a man with one eye called
   Killer Joe McGibbon.
PHIL: Oh, yes. And what's his other eye called?

JUDGE: You are accused of driving up a one-way street.
MOTORIST: Well, I was only going one way.
JUDGE: But didn't you notice the arrows?
MOTORIST: *Arrows*? I didn't even see the Indians.
JUDGE: And where were you going?
MOTORIST: I can't remember – but wherever it was,
   everybody else seemed to be coming back from there!

LITTLE GIRL: Mummy, why are your hands always so soft?

MOTHER: Because I always use wonderful new Snow-bright Liquid for washing my dishes.

LITTLE GIRL: But why does it get your hands so soft?

MOTHER: Because the money Snowbright Liquid pay me for this commercial enables me to buy an automatic dish-washer.

From deepest Africa comes the news that the Globglobs, a tribe of cannibals, have come up with a brand-new food idea.

'We take a human hand,' said a spokesman for the tribe, 'and chop it into small pieces. Then we let this dry in the sun for ten years. After this time, we grind the pieces into powder and place it in bottles and sell it. All you have to do is add milk to the powder. We call it a hand-shake.'

MANAGER: You're late. You should have been here an hour ago.

CLERK: I would have been here on time, but I fell out of a twelfth-storey window.

MANAGER: Well, it doesn't seem to have harmed you.

CLERK: No – luckily the ground broke my fall.

MR HIGGINS: My wife can't decide to go to the West Indies or to the frozen North.

MR WIGGINS: Well, she'll have to decide soon. The holidays are only a week away.

MR HIGGINS: All right – Alaska.

At a refined cocktail party, the Hon. Cecil Flintcomb-Maltravers was horrified when a guest took a deep draught of his drink and then let out a terrifically loud belch which reverberated through the room.

'You cad!' cried the Hon. Cecil. 'How dare you belch in front of my wife!'

'Why?' said the guest. 'Was it her turn?'

How do you make a Swiss roll?
Push him over an Alp.

What do we always expect to find on at the cinema?
The roof.

Once upon a time a Chinese warrior named Ho Flo came to England, and found his way to the Court of King Arthur.

'I would like to join the famous Round Table,' said Ho Flo. 'and be one of your knights.'

'Sorry,' said King Arthur. 'I can't allow that.'

'Why not?' said Ho Flo. 'I am a fearless warrior; strong, and willing to lay down my life for you.'

King Arthur replied: 'Yes, that's very nice. But the thing is, I don't want a chink in my armour.'

What fruit does a newly-wedded couple most resemble?
A green pear (pair).

When is a boat like a heap of snow?
When it is adrift.

Why is a dying man like a cobbler?
Because he gives up his awl, looks to his end, and prepares his sole for the last.

What did the owl and the goat do at the square dance?
The hootenanny.

A very proud mother phoned up a big Sunday newspaper and reported that she'd given birth to seventeen children. The girl at the desk didn't quite catch the message and asked: 'Would you repeat that?

'Not if I can help it,' the woman replied.

Knock-knock.
Who's there?
Theatre.
Theatre who?
Theatre clock news.

Knock-knock.
Who's there?
Woody.
Woody who?
Woody come out if he knew who was knocking?

Why do hens always lay in the daytime?
Because at night they become roosters.

Why is a cow's tail like a swan's neck?
Because it always grows down.

What is a drunkard's final drink?
His bier.

Why is a cat longer at night than in the morning?
Because he is let out at night and taken in in the morning.

A rich American and a rich Arab were boasting about how wealthy their own countries were. The discussion went on for hours, till finally the Arab cried:

'Look, we have so much gold that we could build an exact-scale replica out of gold, exact in every detail, of America! Just think of that – all in solid gold!'

The American merely shrugged. 'Okay, okay – build it. We'll *buy* it from you.'

Why is hunting for honey like a legacy?
Because it is a bee-quest.

A man entered a crowded doctor's waiting-room, fell to the ground, rolled himself into a ball and started tumbling about the room, knocking patients and furniture flying. The noise brought the doctor running out of his surgery. When he saw the man on the floor acting so strangely, the doctor said:

'What on earth's the matter with you?'

'I'm a billiard ball,' said the man.

'Well,' said the doctor. 'You'd better come to the head of the queue!'

4 Richer
4 Better
4 Poorer
4 Worse.....

When a man marries, how many wives does he get?
Sixteen – four richer, four poorer, four better, four worse.

Which reptile is very good at mathematics?
An adder.

Why is the word Yes like a mountain?
Because it is an assent.

What do you get if you cross a cowboy with a popular meal?
Hopalong Casserole.

What is it that is always coming, but never arrives?
Tomorrow – as soon as it arrives, it is today.

SPINSTER: Sometimes I feel like a book.
DUSTMAN: Really? Why's that?
SPINSTER: Well, I guess it comes from being left on the shelf for so long.

Why is a bee-hive like a rotten potato?
A bee-hive is a bee-holder, and a beholder is a spectator, and a specked tater is a rotten potato.

Ned Duffer, the village idiot, went to the optician's to have his eyes tested. The optician told him: 'Sit down, cover your right eye with your right hand and read the chart on the wall.'

Simple Ned sat down and covered his left eye with his right hand. 'No, the right eye,' said the optician. Ned then covered his right eye with his left hand. 'No, no . . .' cried the frustrated optician, then he had an idea. He went away and returned with a cornflakes box and cut a small hole in the front. He put this over Ned's head and ordered him to read – whereupon Ned burst into tears.

'What's the matter now?' said the optician.

'Well,' sobbed Ned. 'I was hoping I'd be able to have horn-rimmed ones like me brothers!'

A man went to a butcher's shop and was horrified to see human legs and arms of all sizes hanging on hooks.

'Why, that's horrible!' he cried.

The butcher scowled at him: 'Well – what did you expect in a family butcher's shop?'

Have you heard the one about...

Anyone for Underwater Tennis?

(And Other Games for the Mentally Discarded)

There are lots of games you can play with jokes and riddles. All you need is a pen, a piece of paper, and a herd of charging buffalo. Here are just a few of the fun-filled games you might want to enjoy, if you like self-punishment:

1. Noughts and Riddles. This game, very popular in Siberia, is played up the chimney. The first player draws a nought in the soot, and the second player has to keep asking riddles till the chimney catches fire. The winner is the first player out of the house.

2. Joke-Jumping. The object here is to tell a joke while you are airborne. A Frenchman, Pierre Poke, holds the record with a twenty-line joke which he told after he'd jumped off the Eiffel Tower. Unfortunately, he couldn't be found afterwards, so he didn't get his prize.

Now you see how many foolish games you can invent, using the following jokes and riddles:

'Excuse me, sire,' said the down-and-out tramp to the millionaire he accosted in the street. 'I've trudged over 100 miles to meet you because I've heard you are the world's kindest and most generous man.'

'Indeed,' said the millionaire. 'And will you be going back the same way?'

'I expect so, sir.'

'Then do me a favour, will you? Just deny that rumour when you get back.'

In a large clothes store in Bond Street there was a very fed-up salesgirl who had been serving a very fussy woman for nearly an hour. After all this time, and having chosen nothing, the woman said:

'I think I would look fabulous in something really *flowing*, don't you?'

'Yes,' muttered the salesgirl. 'Why don't you go jump in the river?'

A little girl called Esme Pipple was taken by her father to a seance. When they arrived, the medium asked Esme if there was anybody she would like to contact and speak to.

'I'd like to speak to my Granny,' said Esme.

'Certainly, my dear,' said the medium, going into a deep trance. He began to moan and talk in a strange voice, saying: 'This is your Granny speaking from Heaven . . . a wonderful place in the skies. Is there anything you'd like to ask me, my child?'

'Yes, Granny,' said Esme. 'What are you doing in Heaven when you're not even dead yet?'

MAN: Will the band play anything I request?
WAITER: Certainly, sir.
MAN: Tell them to play shove-ha'penny.

Could you kill somebody just by throwing eggs at him?
Yes, he would be eggs-terminated.

What occurs in every minute, twice in a moment, and yet never in a thousand years?
The letter 'M'.

How do you get a baby astronaut to sleep?
You rock-et.

1ST MAN: I say, do you know the difference between a postbox and an elephant with gout?

2ND MAN: No, I don't.

1ST MAN: Well, I'm not giving *you* any letters to post.

What wears shoes, but has no feet?
The pavement.

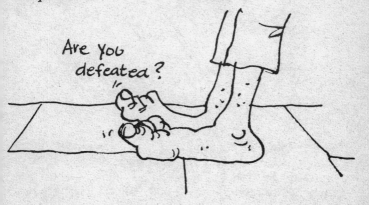

Are you defeated?

POLICEMAN: Here! Why are you trying to cross the road in this dangerous spot? Can't you see there's a zebra crossing only forty yards away?

PEDESTRIAN: Well, I hope the poor beast is having better luck than I am.

The solicitor was reading the late Wilberforce Toeworthy's will, and had just reached the final paragraph. In a deep voice he intoned:

'I always said I'd remember my dear wife, Gertrude, and mention her in my will. So – hello there, Gertie!'

1ST ESKIMO: That's strange. I installed radiators in my kayak and it immediately went up in flames! How do you explain that?

2ND ESKIMO: Simple, my friend. You can't hope to have your kayak and 'eat it!

Why did the prisoner ask for a big mink coat?
Because he was going to spend the night in the cooler.

What is black and white and red all over?
A sunburnt zebra.

How can you check the time without looking at your watch?
Eat an apple and count the pips.

What has four legs and flies?
A dead horse.

Which candles burn longer – wax or tallow?
Neither; both burn shorter.

Why did the spaceman walk?
Because he missed the bus.

Which sea do spaceships sail on?
The Galaxy.

MAN: Waiter, can I have some horrible, greasy chips, an underdone egg, and a steak that tastes like old boot leather cooked in paraffin?

WAITER: I'm sorry, sir, but I'm afraid we couldn't possibly give you anything like that.

MAN: Why not? That's what you gave me yesterday.

A somewhat dreamy character named Hercules Slump went to his doctor and complained of being unable to sleep.

'Can't you sleep at night, then?' said the doctor.

'Oh yes, I sleep very well at night,' said Slump. 'And I sleep quite soundly in the mornings as well. But I find it rather difficult to drop off in the afternoons lately.'

Why did the cow jump over the Moon?
Because there was no other way round.

What's the cheapest way to post somebody?
Stamp on their foot.

What did the astronaut find in his stocking on Christmas Day?
Missile-toe.

'Oh, Doctor, do you mean I'm finally cured?' sighed Maud Pole.

'Yes, Miss Pole,' said the psychiatrist. 'I believe we now have your kleptomania under control and you can go out into the world as normal as anybody.'

'I'm so very grateful,' said Maud Pole. 'I don't know how I'll ever repay you for your help.'

'My fee is adequate,' said the doctor. 'However, should you have a slight relapse, I could do with a small camera and a transistor radio.'

NEWS HEADLINES

The marriage of two lighthouse-keepers in the Orkney Islands was said to be on the rocks.

An Egyptian scientist has invented saw-edged false teeth for eating tinned fruit.

The Government plan to have all meat pies wrapped in tin has been foiled.

Quincey Sprout, MP for Ditheringstone East, took his seat in the House of Commons this morning – but was forced to put it back.

Why is a bachelor such a smart man?
Because he never is miss-taken.

Two singers were about to go on stage to perform their hit song when one of them burst into into a mad fit of coughing.

'Anything wrong, Percy?' said the other.

'I think I've got a frog in my throat, Sidney,' gasped the first.

'Then if I were you,' said Sidney, 'I should let the frog sing – it's got a better voice than you.'

Sid, the cleaner, was alone working in the chemist's shop one evening when the phone rang. He answered with a confident 'Hello!'

'This is Dr Splinter,' said the voice on the telephone. 'Do you have any tincture of trinitrosulphate in aqueous solution?'

'Well, doctor,' said Sid, after a brief pause. 'I'll be quite honest with you. When I said 'Hello!' I told you all I know.'

DAFT QUESTIONS

Is a baby budgerigar called a budget?

A tight budget →

Did the coroner who lost his pub go on an inn quest?
Is an alcoholic ghost a methylated spirit?
Is the Privy Seal a creature with flippers kept in a privy?

If a cat swallows a ball of wool can you expect mittens?

HOSPITAL VISITOR: Your wife Esmeralda misses you a lot, I'll bet.
BANDAGED PATIENT: Oh no, she's a very good shot. That's why I'm here.

After Lord Mousepoke, one of the richest men in the world, died at the age of 105, he was mourned throughout the civilised world. In all the newspapers there were reports of his death, together with details of the £20 million fortune he had left behind him. On a street corner in Edinburgh, one man seemed particularly upset by the news. He was clutching the paper to his chest, moaning and crying: 'He's dead . . . He's dead . . .'

'There, there,' said the newspaper-seller, trying to console him. 'You musn't carry on like that. We've all got to go some time. And Lord Mousepoke wasn't related to you, was he?'

'No,' sobbed the man. 'That's just it!'

76

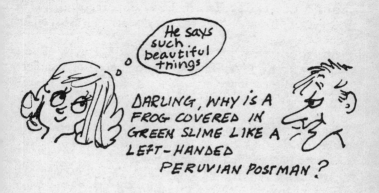

Jokes and Riddles for Swinging Lovers

(*Of Fights and Brawls and Broken Windows*)

Say you've been going out a lot with Sandra Spindle or Hector Wince, and suddenly the sight of their face makes you feel somewhat sick. You can't very well tell them this — but how are you going to stop seeing them? You keep firing relentless rounds of jokes and riddles at them, that's how. Any sweetheart, misty-eyed in the moonlight, aching for a kiss, is bound to think something's wrong if instead of sweet nothings, all her lover whispers in her ear is: 'Darling, why is a frog covered in green slime like a left-handed Peruvian postman?' Now you've got the idea, get your goodbye-baby material from this batch of ludicrous laughs:

GROUND CONTROL: Here is the weather report –
SPACEMAN: I cannot hear you very clearly. Please spell it out.
GROUND CONTROL: W-E-T-H-U-R R-E-P-A-W-T...
SPACEMAN: By Jove! That's the worst spell of weather we've had for a long time ...

'What are you making, Egmont?' asked the woodwork teacher.

'A portable,' replied the small boy.

'A portable what?'

Egmont frowned. 'I'm not really sure, sir. So far I've only made the handles!'

What has two sides, a neck, a bottom and often a broken life?

A bottle.

NEWS HEADLINES

An iron-gate manufacturer in Liverpool was taken to hospital today. He is said to be in an overwrought condition.

A man in Glasgow fell into a vat of beer today and came to a bitter end.

Hens have lost all sense of direction – eggs are going up again.

The President of the International Periscope Manufacturers said in London today that business was looking up.

Owing to a strike at the meteorological office, there will be no weather in Britain tomorrow.

MAN: At last – I've cured my son of biting his nails.
FRIEND: Really? How did you manage that?
MAN: Knocked all his teeth out.

CROSS-BREEDS

What do you get if you cross two parts of the head, one treble-o, and a German?
Ear-tooth-thousand and Hun. (Year 2001).

What do you get if you cross a group of stars with a silver cup?
A constellation prize.

What do you get if you cross a space pistol, a cheer, and a hippopotamus?
A hip-hippo-ray gun.

The pretty young secretary was unable to supply her new boss with any reference. She explained:

'I'm sure my last employer would have given you an excellent one, but unfortunately his wife came into his office, saw me sitting on his lap, and then shot him dead.'

What do you call a space magician?
A flying saucerer.

What children live in the sea?
Buoys and gulls.

TOURIST: Why are you holding that piece of rope up in the air, old man?
RUSTIC: Arrrr, it's my weather guide, sir.
TOURIST: *Weather guide*? But how on earth can you tell the weather with just a piece of rope?
RUSTIC: Well, sir, when it swings about, I know it's windy, and when it's soaking wet, I know it's rainy.

The very fat woman turned to the man sitting next to her in the bus and said in a loud voice:

'If you were a gentleman, you'd stand up and let one of those women sit down.'

'And if you were a lady,' said the man, 'you'd get up and let all four of them sit down.'

What turned the moon pale?
At-mos-fear.

Who is the meanest man in the world?
The man who finds a crutch, then breaks his leg so he can use it.

Why do witches fly through the air on broomsticks?
Because vacuum cleaners are too heavy.

It will never fly...

'Is that the police?' cried a panic-stricken voice on the phone to the police headquarters.

'Yes, this is the police station.'

'Oh, thank goodness! I want to report a burglar trapped in an old lady's bedroom. Please come quickly!'

'And who is that calling?' said the policeman.

'The burglar!'

PSYCHIATRIST: And what seems to be the trouble?

PATIENT: Well, doctor, I keep having this tremendous urge to paint myself all over with gold paint.

PSYCHIATRIST: Mmmm . . . I think we can safely say that you are suffering from a gilt complex.

What do you get if you plant an electric light bulb in space?

A rocket from the Electricity Board.

Who carries the broom in a football team?
The sweeper.

Which King was entirely covered with thick hair?
King Kong.

A magician on board a cruise ship used to do amazing tricks every night in the cabaret – but the captain's pet parrot always used to shout 'Phoney! Phoney!' at the end of the magician's act.

Then one day the ship hit an iceberg and sank. But the magician and the parrot managed to cling to a piece of wood and float clear of the sinking ship.

After a few hours of floating around, the parrot turned to the magician and said: 'Okay, genius, I give up. What have you done with the ship?'

A woman couldn't get her alarm clock to go, so she took it to a small jeweller's shop owned by a German.

'Will you mend this for me, please?' said the woman.

'Certainly, madam,' said the man. When she had left he took the clock into a back room, tied it to a chair and hissed at it in a sinister way: 'Come now ... start verking. Ve haf vays of making you tock ...'

Knock-knock.
Who's there?
Jupiter.
Jupiter who?
Jup-etter hurry or you'll miss the train.

Knock-knock.
Who's there?
Aries.
Aries who?
Aries a tavern in the town, in the town ...

MAN: In your sermon this morning, vicar, you said it was wrong for a person to profit from other people's mistakes. Do you really agree with that?
VICAR: Of course I do.
MAN: In that case, would you mind refunding the twenty pounds I paid you for marrying me to my wife eleven years ago?

What can you make that nobody can see?
A noise.

1ST MAN: I heard you were moving your piano, so I came to help.

2ND MAN: Thanks a lot, but I got it upstairs already.

1ST MAN: Did you do it alone?

2ND MAN: No, I hitched the budgie to it.

1ST MAN: But how on earth could a tiny budgie haul a grand piano up two flights of stairs?

2ND MAN: Easy – I used a whip.

INTERVIEWER: Excuse my asking, but what are those tiny little bongos hanging from your ears?

POP-STAR: Oh, they're just my ear-drums.

What trees have neither leaves or bark?
Shoe-trees.

What can travel at the speed of sound, but has neither legs, wings, nor engines?
ur voice.

How do you write a letter to a fish?
Just drop him a line.

NEWS HEADLINES

Under a new pay award, barbers are to get more fringe benefits.

Speaking about the droppings of pigeons in the town of Clumpthorpe, the mayor said: 'We must not try and dodge the issue.'

Eleven tons of human hair was stolen from a factory in West Fliptown this morning. Police are combing the area.

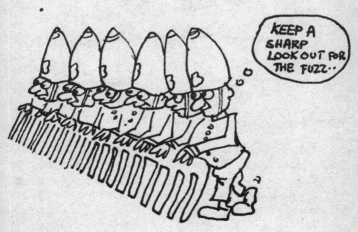

TOURIST: Excuse my asking, but why have they built that enormous fifty-foot fence around this graveyard?

PARSON: Ah, that's because so many people are simply dying to get in.

PATIENT: Give it to me straight, Doctor – have I got very long to live?

DOCTOR: It's very difficult to say, Mr Sprout. But if I were you, I wouldn't start reading any serials.

1ST MAN: My pet anaconda snake plays chess with me.

2ND MAN: That's amazing! It must be a really intelligent snake.

1ST MAN: Not really – I've won five games to two so far this week.

An aspiring variety artiste walked into an agent's office looking for work. The agent said: 'What do you do?'

Without a word, the artiste lifted up his arms, flew around the office, out of the window, across the street and back in through the window, making a perfect two-point landing in front of the agent's desk.

'Okay, okay,' said the agent. 'So you do bird impersonations . . . anything else?'

1ST IDIOT: What's that iron box for?
2ND IDIOT: That's my pillow.
1ST IDIOT: Pillow? Won't it be a bit hard?
2ND IDIOT: Do you think I'm crazy? I'm going to stuff it with straw first.

A swimmer came out of the sea, blue and shivering with cold, and headed for a refreshment kiosk nearby.

'Coff—ff—ee,' he stuttered.

'Certainly,' said the assistant. 'Milk and sugar?'

'It doesn't matter,' said the swimmer. 'I'm only going to pour it over my feet!'

Stick 'Em Up!

(And Other Methods of Getting Attention)

To be able to tell a joke properly, you need a good audience. It's no good telling a joke to a tree (trees seldom laugh, except when their top bough is tickled with a chainsaw). So you need to be able to grab the attention of your audience immediately and then commence the joking. Here are a few ways to do this:

1. Render the audience unconscious with this book, then joke away.
2. In a loud voice shout 'I am the Bright-White Super-Soap Jester and I will give £5 to the first person to answer this riddle . . .'
3. Enlist the aid of a ground-to-earth missile.
4. Rescue somebody from drowning, or a burning chocolate biscuit factory, and when being interviewed by the press, slip your joke in.

If all these methods fail, don't despair. Tell your joke or riddle to any park litter bin; they have great senses of humour. There follows a section of jokes approved by (and found in) park litter bins.

91

Why is a cowardly soldier like butter?
Both are yellow and run when exposed to fire.

Where are there no fat people?
Finland.

Where do cowboys keep their supply of water?
In their ten-gallon hats.

Which fish go to heaven when they die?
Angel fish.

What's the best thing to take when you are run over?
The car's number.

CROSS-BREEDS

What do you get if you cross a round black hat with a rocket?
A very fast bowler.

What do you get if you cross the Moon with the top of a house?
A lun-attic.

What do you get if you cross a miserable man with a space-ship?
A moan-rocket.

'Sebastian!' shouted the editor of the newspaper. 'Did you get the story about the man who sings bass and soprano at the same time?'

'Ah, there was no story there, sir,' said the young reporter. 'It turned out that the man had two heads . . .'

Why are people who read on train journeys very clever?
Because they can read between the lines.

What do they call it when a prisoner has plastic surgery?
A con-version.

What box can never hold a secret?
A chatterbox.

What game do judges play?
Tennis – because it's played on courts.

When was it always wet in France?
When the monarchs were reigning.

REPORTER: Is it true that you actually landed on the Moon?

SPACEMAN: Yes, that's right.

REPORTER: But you were unable to stay there. Can you tell us why that was?

SPACEMAN: Well, there was no room! You see, it was a full moon.

CUSTOMER: I say, ironmonger, have you got one-inch nails?

IRONMONGER: Yes, sir.

CUSTOMER: Then scratch my back, will you? It's itching something awful.

JUDGE: Constable, do you recognise this woman?

CONSTABLE: Yes, m'lud. She came up to me when I was in plain clothes and tried to pass this five-pound note off on me.

JUDGE: Counterfeit?

CONSTABLE: Yes, m'lud. She had two.

Why did the beatnik chicken cross the road?
Because it was a lay-about.

REPORTER: Did you find any animals on the Moon?

SPACEMAN: Yes, we did find one – called a gnu.

REPORTER: A gnu? That's rather an odd animal to find on the Moon, isn't it?

SPACEMAN: Oh, I don't know. Surely you've heard of a gnu moon?

MAN: Just how does it feel to hurtle through space?
SPACEMAN: It hurtles!

Which trees do hands grow on?
Palm trees.

Who designed the first raincoat?
Anna Rack.

Why did the ape put a piece of steak on his head?
Because he thought he was a griller (gorilla).

GUS: Where's your dog?
SID: I had to have it put down.
GUS: That's a shame. Was it mad?
SID: Well, it wasn't exactly pleased.

Zebedee Merryacre was on holiday in Egypt. While he was there, he decided to visit the local bazaar.

'Want to buy the genuine skull of Moses?' a stall-owner asked him.

'Not really,' said Zebedee. 'It's too expensive.'

'Then how about this skull?' said the stall-owner, producing another one. 'This is much cheaper, because it's smaller – the genuine skull of Moses as a child!'

DOCTOR'S RECEPTIONIST: You'll find Dr Prout very funny – he'll have you in stitches.
PATIENT: I sincerely hope not. I only dropped in for a check-up.

What did Little John say when Robin Hood fired at him?
That was an arrow escape.

Why is an elephant an unwelcome guest?
Because he always brings his trunk with him.

Why can't a bicycle stand up for very long?
Because it's two-tyred.

Why is it useless to send a telegram to Washington?
Because he's dead.

Why did the ocean roar?
Because it had lobsters in its bed.

STREET SELLER: Like to buy a nice tie?
MAN: How much is it?
STREET SELLER: Ten pence.
MAN: Mmmm, that's cheap. What colour is it?
STREET SELLER: Sssshhhh! The man next to you is still
   wearing it!

BOSS: Miss Shrubshaw – why are you late again this morning?

TYPIST: I overslept.

BOSS: Good gracious – you mean you sleep at home as *well*?

When does a man become two men?
When he is beside himself.

Why should a savage dog always be a hungry man's best friend?
Because he's sure to give him a bite.

Why didn't they bury the Duke of Wellington with full military honours in 1847?
Because he didn't die until 1852.

What's the best way to find a liar out?
Go to his house when he isn't in.

What did the beaver say to the tree?
So long, it's been nice to gnaw you.

Why do people always put their right shoe on first?
Because it would be stupid to put their wrong shoe on first.

Hector Waterbound, being an idiot, decided to have a brain transplant. He went along to the hospital and was given the choice of two brains – an architect's for £50 and a politician's brain for £1,000.

'Does that mean the politician's brain is much better than the architect's?' asked Hector.

'Not necessarily,' said the brain transplant salesman, 'it's just that the politician's brain has never been used.'

Why did the man become an electrician?
He was looking for a bit of light relief.

Why does the Lord Mayor of London wear red, white and blue braces?
To keep his trousers up.

What's the best way to get into the puppetry business?
Pull a few strings.

What did the first tonsil say to the second tonsil?
The doctor's taking me out tonight.

A Thousand Different Uses for Jokes and Riddles

(Not Including Washing Down Your Dirty Bathtub)

Don't think that jokes and riddles are just for making people laugh, or making people ill. Far from it. Their shock-value alone can be very therapeutic. Here's just a selection of their countless uses:

1. As an anaesthetic for a patient undergoing funny-bone surgery.
2. As a small, nearly white flag of cowardice.
3. As material for a serious essay about air-pollution on Venus.
4. As an incredibly badly-forged £1 note.
5. As a billiard ball for inept players.
6. As a back-scratcher.
7. As treatment for a person who's had too much laughing-gas.

Now – just add nine hundred and ninety three more, and you'll have a thousand uses for jokes and riddles.

MAN: Good morning, I wonder if you can help me: my house is overrun with mice. Do you have any poison that will get rid of them?

CHEMIST: No sir, I'm afraid we're sold out. Why not try Boots?

MAN: Don't be stupid – I want to poison them, not kick them to death!

Why is a daily paper like an army?
Because it has leaders, columns and reviews.

The young man walked into the pet-shop and asked if he could buy 177 cockroaches, 55 beetles, 21 mice and 7 rats.

'I'm sorry sir, but we can only supply the mice,' said the owner of the pet-shop. 'But out of interest, what on earth do you want all those other creatures for?'

'Well, I got evicted from my flat this morning,' replied the young man. 'And the landlord said that I must leave the place exactly as I found it.'

A man rushed into a pub in a highly agitated state. 'Does anybody own a great big black cat with a white collar?' he said, in a nervous voice. There was no reply.

'Well, does anybody *know* of a large black cat with a white collar?' asked the man again, raising his voice above the general noise of the bar. But still nobody answered his question.

'Oh dear,' muttered the man. 'I think I've just run over the vicar.'

When does a fire flare up?
When it is bellowed at.

'Darling – will you marry me?' asked romance-stricken Bertie Byron, getting down on his knees and offering his girl a glittering ring.

'Oooo, Bert,' whispered Dorothea Hedge, 'are they *real* diamonds?'

'I hope so,' said Bertie Byron. 'Because if they aren't, I've been swindled out of a pound!'

What did the big cracker say to the little cracker?
My pop is bigger than your pop.

Knock-knock.
Who's there?
Adolf.
Adolf who?
A dolf ball hid me in der mouf ad dat's why I dalk funny.

Knock-knock.
Who's there?
You're a lady.
You're a lady who?
Hey, I didn't know you could yodel.

What passes under the sun without casting a shadow?
A breeze.

Where does one keep one's underwear when travelling?
In a brief-case.

Which animal is it best to be on a cold day?
A little otter.

What's the best kind of car to get drunk in?
A saloon car.

Why is language referred to as the mother tongue?
Because father seldom gets the chance to use it.

What do you do if somebody offers you a rock cake?
Take your pick.

One day the lion woke up and went for a prowl in the jungle. Soon he came across a snake. 'Who is the king of the jungle?' he said.

'You, of course,' said the snake.

Next the lion met a monkey, and asked it: 'Who is the king of the jungle?'

'Why, you are,' shivered the monkey.

This went on all day, all the animals agreeing that the lion was the king of the jungle. Then the lion came across an elephant.

'Who is the king of the jungle?' said the lion.

In reply, the elephant picked up the lion with its trunk, hurled the lion around in the air, then bashed him against the ground and stamped up and down on him.

'All right, all right,' groaned the battered lion. 'There's no need to lose your temper just because you don't know the answer!'

What did the circus owner say to the naughty elephant?
Pack your trunk and get out.

Knock-knock.
Who's there?
Irish stew.
Irish stew who?
Irish stew in the name of the law.

The medical lecturer in the newly opened medical school turned to one of his pupils and said:

'Now, Poppingpepper, it's clear from this X-ray I am holding up that one of this patient's legs is considerably shorter than the other. This of course accounts for the patient's habit of falling over. But what would *you* do in a case like this?'

Poppingpepper thought for a while, then said: 'I should imagine, sir, that I'd keep falling over, too.'

When is a trilby hat like a thorough spanking?
When it is felt.

Why should a sailor know where giant toads live?
Because he's been to sea (see).

The man entered the shoe-shop in a furious temper. He found the salesman and snarled: 'Look – about this pair of shoes you sold me last week. One of them has a heel at least two inches shorter than the other. What do you expect me to do?'

The salesman calmly replied: 'Limp, sir. Limp.'

'Darling, do you love me?' sighed Sadie.
'Of course I do,' sighed Sidney.
'Darling, whisper something soft and sweet in my ear.'
'Lemon meringue pie . . .'

When is water musical?
When it's piping hot.

1ST MAN: Why are you so angry?
2ND MAN: Oh, it's all the rage now.

On a walking holiday in Ireland, an old couple found themselves at dusk one evening on a lonely road with no sign of the town where they had arranged to spend the night. After some time they spied a man and a woman rounding up their sheep, so they asked them how far the town was.

'Well, now,' said the shepherd. 'It's a good five miles.'

His wife, seeing the tourists' faces fall, whispered: 'Sure, Patrick, make it two miles – they look awful tired.'

Why did the dog howl?
Because he barked up
the wrong tree.

Why is a horse very clever?
Because he can eat his dinner without a bit in his mouth.

For twenty-five years, old Agatha Moon's pet parrot had not said a single word. She was convinced that it was a stupid bird, unable to learn a word of English. One day, though, as she was feeding it a piece of lettuce, the parrot suddenly squawked:

'Ughh – take it away! There's a *maggot* on it!'

'Why, you can talk!' gasped Agatha. 'But why haven't you talked in all the twenty-five years I've had you?'

'Well,' said the parrot, 'the food's been excellent up till now.'

Riddles Without any Answers

(For Bunglers Without Any Brains)

Some people manage to do *everything* wrong. You know the type – they post letters in bus windows, eat packets then throw away the contents, turn up for school just as the bell is ringing for everybody to go home, watch television with their backs to the screen, read papers upside down, and swap their stamp collection for something stupid, like a champion slug, or a pet rock. Worse still, they always forget the answers to riddles.

Well, this chapter is especially for those people. For none of the riddles has an answer, so they can't possibly be wrong. Even now, they'll probably goof and start eating the chapter instead of reading it, but at least we've done our best to help them.

1. Why did the bishop hide the British Museum?.

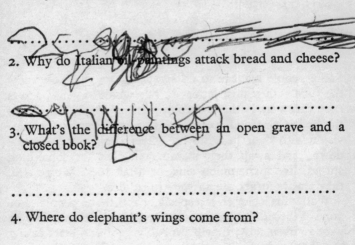

2. Why do Italian oil paintings attack bread and cheese?

3. What's the difference between an open grave and a closed book?

4. Where do elephant's wings come from?

116

5. When did the nostril quiver and burst into flames?

6. Why do oak trees walk in their sleep?

7. How many languages can a dustbin speak?

....

8. What sort of view would you get from inside a fish-paste jar?

....

9. What has eleven heads, four baked beans, two hands, five pairs of pyjamas and keeps shouting 'Look out – they've gone!'

....

10. When is a jar not a jar?

....

11. Why do slugs dance the polka on September 25th?

· ·

CHILE KNEES

THE ANDES

12. How many knees has South America?

· ·

13. What have St Paul's Cathedral and bubble-gum in common?

· ·

14. Why did the skull rattle at tea-time?

· ·

15. What's the difference between Cleopatra's Needle and the North Korean cricket team?

. . . .

16. When do Australian trees turn bright blue?

. . . .

17. What's the difference between Mount Etna and Aunt Maud?

. . . .

18. How can you climb a newspaper without anybody noticing you?

. . . .

19. What has 106 ears, a toffee apple up its nose and a beard equipped with stereophonic sound?

. . . .

20. What did the piranha fish say to the drunken tulip?

. . . .

Riddles Without Question

(For Quiz-Kids Without Skid-Lids)

Here's a quiz to make your brains fizz. Before you are the answers to 20 *real* riddles — what you have to do is supply the missing questions. Take your time and think (there's a time limit of 25 years, though, so don't fall asleep too often). After the quiz you'll find the missing questions, unless they're lost. Rate yourself as follows regarding how many you got right:

15 – 20 Correct: Brazen liar!

10 – 15 Correct: Braggart and answer-peeker!

2 – 10 Correct: That's more like it.

    1 Correct: Seems like your mind is on holiday.

    0 Correct: Are you sure you're looking at the end of the right *chapter*?

1 ....

The source (sauce) and the currents.

2 ....

Because it saw the sky-lark.

3 ....

Well, well, well.

4 ....

Because it is a bawl-room (ballroom).

5 ... .

A squawker.

6 ....

Shredded tweet.

7 ....

Stand beside a fan.

8 ....

The tide.

9 ....

A boxer.

10 ....

Hey, you're far too young to smoke!

11 ....

To the dock (doc).

12 ....

Between you and me there's something that smells.

13 ....

A lavender bush.

14 . . . .

When they realised how green they were.

15 . . . .

Because he is a refuse man.

16 . . . .

A cabbage.

17 . . . .

Mount Ever-rest.

18 . . . .

When the wind makes them rock.

19 ....

Miss Ouri and Mrs Sippi.

20 ....

Thigh-length boots.

Questions

HOW!

1. What parts of a river can be eaten?
2. Why did the sun-beam?
3. What do they call three deep damp holes in the ground?
4. Why is a children's nursery a good place for dancing?
5. What do they call a Red Indian baby?
6. What would you have if your lawnmower ran over a bird?
7. How do you keep cool at a hot football match?
8. What comes in without knocking?
9. Which dog will find you in a ring?
10. What did the big chimney say to the tiny chimney?
11. Where do sick ships go to?
12. What did the right eye say to the left eye?
13. What bush has good sense (scents)?
14. When did the tomatoes turn red?
15. Why will the dustman never accept an invitation?
16. What stands on one leg with its heart in its head?
17. Which is the laziest mountain in the world?
18. How do trees become petrified?
19. Who are the two biggest women in America?
20. What's the best thing to wear with purple, yellow, black, blue and orange striped socks?

Here are some of the most recent titles in our exciting fiction series:

☐ Pursuit of the Deadly Diamonds *J. J. Fortune* £1.25
☐ A Leader in the Chalet School *Elinor M. Brent-Dyer* £1.50
☐ Voyage of Terror *J. H. Brennan* £1.75
☐ The Witch Tree Symbol *Carolyn Keene* £1.50
☐ The Clue in the Broken Blade *Franklin W. Dixon* £1.25
☐ The Mystery of the Purple Pirate *William Arden* £1.25
☐ Chestnut Gold *Patricia Leitch* £1.25
☐ Monsters of the Marsh *David Tant* £1.75

Armadas are available in bookshops and newsagents, but can also be ordered by post.

HOW TO ORDER
ARMADA BOOKS, Cash Sales Dept., GPO Box 29, Douglas, Isle of Man, British Isles. Please send purchase price plus 15p per book (maximum postal charge £3.00). Customers outside the UK also send purchase price plus 15p per book. Cheque, postal or money order — no currency.

NAME (Block letters) _____

ADDRESS _____

_____

_____

While every effort is made to keep prices low, it is sometimes necessary to increase prices on short notice. Armada Books reserve the right to show new retail prices on covers which may differ from those previously advertised in the text or elsewhere.